CHE

FOR BEGINNERS™

AF668387

Sergio Sinay

Illustrated by

Miguel Angel Scenna

Orient BlackSwan

CHE FOR BEGINNERS

ORIENT BLACKSWAN PRIVATE LIMITED

Registered Office
3-6-752 Himayatnagar, Hyderabad 500 029 (A.P.), INDIA
e-mail: centraloffice@orientblackswan.com

Other Offices
Bangalore, Bhopal, Bhubaneshwar, Chennai, Ernakulam, Guwahati, Hyderabad, Jaipur, Kolkata, Lucknow, Mumbai, New Delhi, Patna

Cover Design: Susetta Bozzi

Published by arrangement with
Writers and Readers Limited
P O Box 29522
London N1 8 FB

First published in India by
Orient Longman Private Limited 2002
Reprinted 2006
First Orient Blackswan impression 2010

ISBN 13: 978 81 250 2234 3
ISBN 10: 81 250 2234 1

Printed in India at
Glorious Printers
Delhi

Published by
Orient Blackswan Private Limited
1/24 Asaf Ali Road
New Delhi 110 002
e-mail: delhi@orientblackswan.com

Publisher's Preface

The mysteries and uncertainties surrounding Che Guevera's life and death bring to mind the Chinese box-within-a-box (within a box). You open a box expecting to find an answer...instead of an answer, you find another box. It is the complex, layered reality of Latin America. No linear once-upon-a-time storytelling could do it justice. So a handful of brilliant Latin American novelists invented a style called Magic Realism.

Sergio Sinay, the Argentinian author of Che For Beginners™, tells Che's story in the tradition of the great Latin American novelists. At times the story seems to be told by a fortune teller, foreseeing the future. At times, the events of Che's life reverberate backward into the past, forward into the future, or "horizontally," on a collision course with other Larger-than-Life fates...like JFK.

CHE FOR BEGINNERS™ mirrors Che's life, at once brutally realistic and almost religiously mythic. (Take another look at the photographs of the dead Che: There is something spiritual about them; even if you don't like Che's politics, it's hard to shake the feeling that you are looking at something akin to a secular saint.)

Bios

SERGIO SINAY

Sergio Sinay is an Argentine journalist and writer. He has directed important publications, won La Nación newspaper's Essay Prize. He coordinates masculine identity groups. He also wrote Gestalt for Beginners.

MIGUEL ANGEL SCENNA

Miguel Angel Scenna is an Argentine artist specializing in historical comics. He worked for the Clarín newspaper and other important publications. He also illustrated Sai Baba for Beginners.

In the Heart of South America...

Bolivia, a country of seven-and-a-half million people, is located in the Andes Mountains in the heart of South America. Although for years, like much of South America, Bolivia was ruled by Spain, 42% of its population is still of Indian origin. In 1825, Bolivia won its independence and advanced pre-Conquest civilizations flourished on its land. Tin, silver, copper and zinc are its main resources.

Thanks to tin exports, the country thrived up to the second decade of the twentieth century. In 1932 President Salamanca (who reached power by a popular revolt) declared war on Paraguay. Known as the Chaco War, the result was a disaster for Bolivia, with thousands of casualties and important territorial losses.

By 1897 Bolivia had lost its only ocean outlet to Chile during the Pacific War. Since 1937, the country suffered a succession of military coups and peasant revolts. The central government was not restored until 1985, during Victor Paz Estenssoro's second rule.

The capital of Bolivia is La Paz, a city enclaved in a basin 10,800 feet above sea level. 480 miles southwest of La Paz lies Vallegrande.

Vallegrande, a small settlement with about twenty thousand inhabitants, is a typical plateau village, spread out on a wild terrain, watched over by mountains and haunted by a nearby jungle.

They had been searching the ground with their shovels for two weeks. They looked tired. Those around them—military and civilians—were anxious and tense beneath the ruthless sun.

GOT SOMETHING HERE!
THERE'S MORE!

29 years earlier, in the same region...

On reaching the El Yuro canyon, they were exposed to view and to sudden ambush.
CRACK
TRAK
TRAK

With no way out, no choice, 20 men hidden in the jungle started what would be their last combat.
Their leader is someone the rangers know as Commander Ramon.

As the hours goes by, the struggle grows increasingly fierce. Though the forces are drastically uneven—185 government soldiers to 20 guerrillas—the guerrillas put up a heroic fight.

It's the beginning of the end. Some of the men hidden in the thicket manage to escape.

Others fall under the bullets and bayonets.

At 7 PM, the sun set on the end of the battle. Four soldiers and five rebels were dead.

An officer, Captain Gary Prado, approaches one of the wounded rebels. It's Commander Ramon.
BUT...

DON'T SHOOT...
I AM CHE!

I'M MORE VALUABLE TO YOU ALIVE THAN DEAD...

Captain Prado calls his men...

...meanwhile Captain Prado sends a coded message that Bolivian superior officers have been hoping for, for months.

39 Years Earlier in Rosario, Argentina

Rosario, the third largest city in Argentina, is located on the right bank of the Parana River. It has some 1,100,000 inhabitants and a university founded in 1730. The city, a trading port for crops and livestock, boomed in the 40 s and 50 s. A commercial hub, the metallurgic, paper, oil and agricultural industries also flourished.

On June 14, 1928, student demonstrators had taken over the School of Medicine at Rosario. Now, ten years later, they celebrated the tenth anniversary of the Reform, a program that had won equal rights for students, alumni, and professors. They were now in the process of demanding the University Council's resignation.

In a nearby maternity hospital, a woman endures and enjoys a unique and unforgettable moment in her life.

She and her husband, architect Ernesto Guevara Lynch, would have four other children (Roberto, Celia, Ana Maria and Juan Martin), but none would impact twentieth century history like this little one, christened Ernesto Guevara.

According to the ancient Chinese horoscope, the child was born under the sign of the Dragon, the most ambitious of all signs, a seeker of ideals, venerated, respected and gifted with a unique talent: to be born and to die a thousand times in one lifetime. The Dragon, Chinese wisemen say, protects, is brave and capable of undergoing any venture. He bets on all or nothing. He fears no death; he knows he will resurge from his ashes.

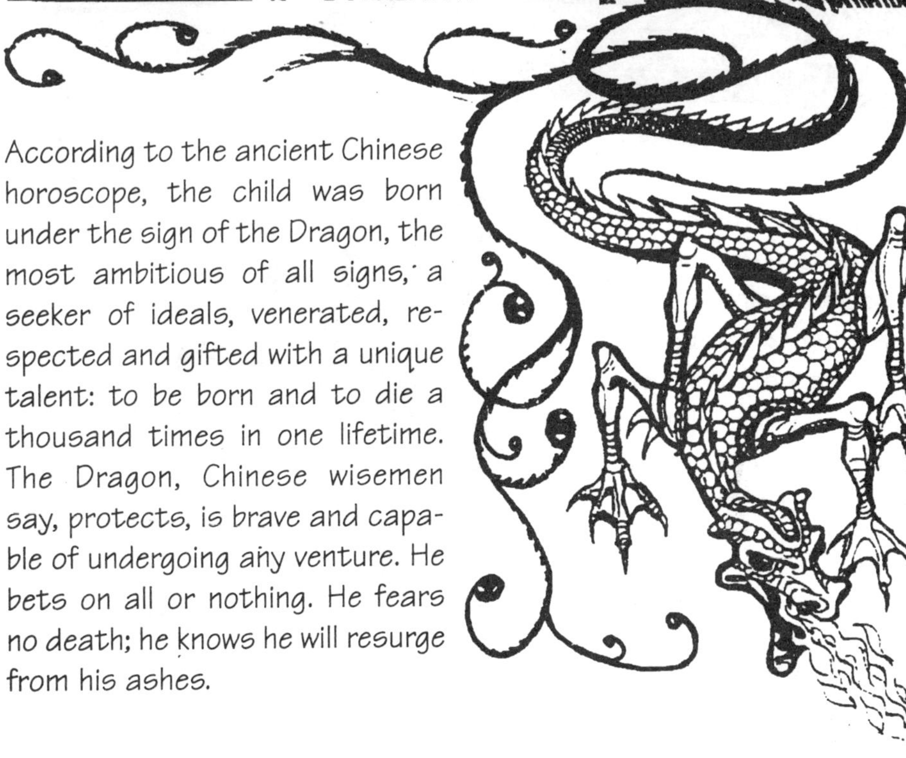

From the beginning, journeys and change marked his life. Shortly before his birth, his parents had moved to Caraquati, in Misiones. His father bought a yerba mate* plantation but it did not work out. After selling it, the family moved to San Isidro, by the Rio de la Plata.
May 2 of 1930 was a cold and rainy day. In spite of the weather, Celia de la Serna went swimming at the San Isidro Boat Club, as her young son slept by the pool...
* Paraguayan tea
THIS BOY HAS ASTHMA.
That night, the 23-month-old boy woke with a high fever and had great difficulty breathing. He seemed to have a strong flu. The neighborhood doctor came to see him and diagnosed the disease that would haunt Ernesto throughout his life...

At the time asthma was a dreaded disease. For two years Ernesto received all kinds of treatments, but nothing helped. The family made a decision.

Alta Gracia is a beautiful highland town, 19 miles from the city of Cordoba. Ernesto's brothers and sisters would be born there, while he made friends and began to show the first signs of a natural leader.

In those early days, distinct personality traits start showing up...

Also in those days, the children get some advice from their father they will not forget.

Ernesto Guevara Lynch's words were timely: On September 6, 1930, General Jos Felix Uriburu overthrew the government. After imprisoning democratically elected President Hipolito Yrigoyen, General Uriburu initiated a period in Argentine history called "The Infamous Decade." For the next half of a century, the military would repeatedly violate the Constitution and establish de facto regimes.

In the cruel and uncertain years that followed, violence became a way of life. The Argentine Civic Legion—a Fascist group—routinely committed political murders. On April 9 of 1931, the legendary anarchist Severino Digiovanni was executed by a firing squad...

...In Congress, Santa Fe senator Lisandro de la Torre denounced outrageous meat swindles that benefitted British interests. During one of these debates, on July 23, 1935, an official bodyguard killed senator Lorenzo Bordabehere, de la Torre's comrade and friend. Frustrated by corruption, de la Torre would kill himself in 1939.

Things go no better elsewhere in the world. Between 1936 and 1939, a civil war bleeds Spain. Francisco Franco, calling himself "Leader of Spain by God's Grace", defeats the democratic Republican forces. Ruthless and authoritarian, he would keep the country in the Dark Ages for decades.

In Germany, **Adolf Hitler** has been consolidating concentrated State and Government power since 1934. Gradually but brutally he wipes out the opposition and the unions, starts a Jewish extermination campaign under the guise of Aryan racial "purity" and convinces people that war will solve Germany's economic crisis. In September of 1939, he sets off the fiercest conflagration humanity has yet known: **World War II.**

In 1940, in the midst of the war—during which Argentina took a neutralist stance—Ernesto entered Dean Funes National School*, in Córdoba, where he began his secondary education. There he would not be an honors student, but a unique one, nonetheless.

* Patterned on the French lycee, the Argentine school is not the same as US high school. It offers five years of rigorous classical training following seven years of elementary schooling.

During those years he stood out as a rugby player for the Cordoba Estudiantes Club. Growing up robust and agile, asthma was little more than a minor irritation...

On January 11, 1943, General Justo died and Vice-president Ramon S. Castillo assumed rule. While Ernesto attended his third year of secondary school, another military coup overthrew Castillo on June 4th, 1943, and a pro-Nazi government led by General Ramírez seized control. Meanwhile, another military man started attracting attention, because of his overtures to blue collar workers who feel left out...

...in 1946, after being Labor Secretary and Vice-president, this Colonel, Juan Domingo Peron, won the election on February 24, and changed Argentine history. "Peronism" became a massive populist movement. The most progressive variants pursued State capitalism. The most retrogressive would generate a terrorist band in the 70's known as The Triple A (Argentine Anticommunist Alliance).

At the Guevara de La Sernas' household, both the conservative and the socialist groups of the family opposed Peron, someone they saw as a by-product of Fascism and Francoism. On August 25, 1946, 16 year-old Ernesto, along with his family, celebrated the end of the war and the defeat of Nazism on the streets of Córdoba.

1946 was also the year of Ernesto's first love. María del Carmen Ferreyra (Chichina), a rich rancher's daughter, felt the spark, too.

Romance began, but it lacked the Ferreyra's blessing...

A new family move left this first love behind. In 1946, the family moved to Buenos Aires, where Ernesto enrolled in the University School of Medicine and played rugby for the San Isidro Club.

The humidity of Buenos Aires revived his asthma and ignited his vigorous traveling spirit. During the summer he set out as a sailor on a Merchant Fleet ship "to get to know other countries." On disembarking a month later, he felt frustrated:

Meanwhile, he spent a lot of time sipping mate* and playing chess, two of his eternal passions. He also found time for his studies...

* Convivial mate: a strong brew of Paraguayan tea passed from hand to hand in any gathering.

...and for planning new adventures. Shortly after his 20th birthday, he connected a small engine to his bike and hit the road to cover the country. His itinerary was vast and intense. He headed north, toward the mountains. He traveled 2,480 miles, covering 12 provinces, where he saw both wealth and poverty. Something other than a simple adventurous spirit started growing within him...

As Ernesto's mother recovered (after a breast cancer tumor is removed), the Guevara's home became an active hub for anti-Peronist militants. Ernesto watched and listened to everything...

During that time, he met socialist and communist students opposed to Peron's government. Later, he would devour poetry and become a Neruda fan.

* Alpargatas is a low-priced canvas shoe with rope soles, a symbol of the vindication of the lower classes that Peron used as a political weapon during his rule.

Meanwhile in Cordoba, Alberto Granados, a 28 year-old childhood friend of the Guevaras, told his younger brother Tom about an old dream.

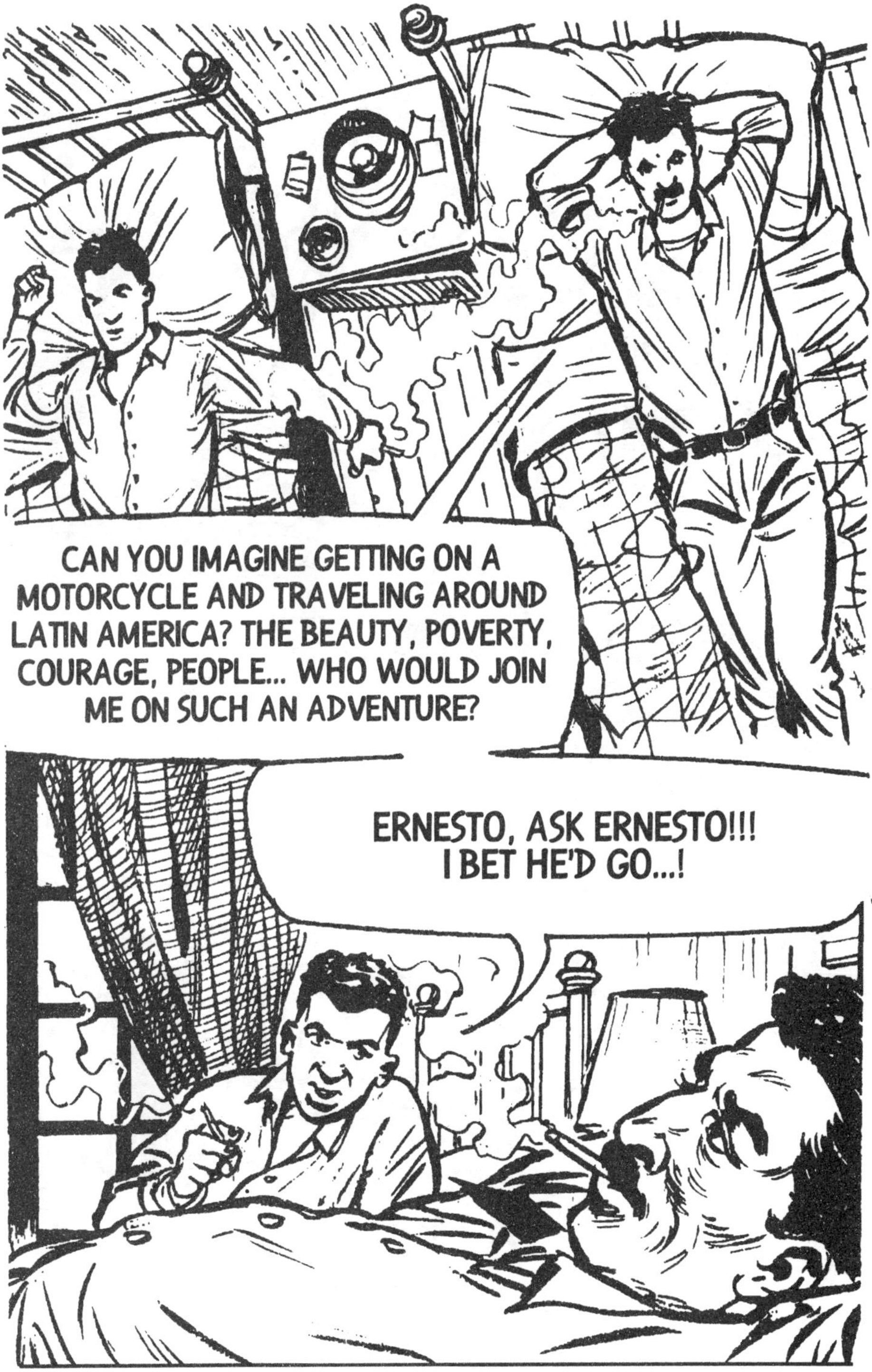

On December 29 of 1951, Granados and Ernesto set out on an old motorcycle called La Poderosa II (The Powerful II).

They crossed the Andes range from the south and headed up towards Santiago while taking turns driving. Later, Ernesto would remember: "The bike puffed as from boredom and so we did as from exhaustion".

Before getting to Santiago fate, in the form of defective brakes, intervened to force a slight change of plans...

Afterwards in his memoirs, Ernesto would write: "That was it for La Poderosa II. We turned from motorized borrowers into unmotorized borrowers".

They took to traveling on trucks, by foot, as train cops. They lodged wherever they could. They worked to survive: their goal was to keep on going.

The trip continued across South America, as did the experiences. They visited the remains of Machu Pichu in Peru and the leper shelters in the jungle.

From the Peruvian jungle they went up the Amazon on a raft, crossed Brazilian territory, became occasional soccer players in Colombia and on the 14th of July 1952, they found themselves in Caracas, Venezuela...

There the shared journey came to an end. Granados received an offer to work in a lepers' shelter (his great dream), while Ernesto had to keep the promise he'd made to his mother:-to go back and graduate as a physician. Ernesto intended to get home via a plane carrying horses via Buenos Aires-Caracas-Miami-Maracaibo-Buenos Aires. He intended to fly to Miami and from there, by a complicated route, to Argentina.

But, once again, fate in the form of mechanical failure intervened: The plane was held up in Miami, so Ernesto wandered about with Jaime Jimmy Roca, a Cordobean friend he ran into.

Stuck in Miami, Ernesto meets Puerto Ricans, Guatemalans, Cubans...

About the middle of 1953 he graduates and plans: to go back to Venezuela to work in the leper shelter with Granados. But his lack of funds called for a less ambitious goal: He and his friend Carlos Calica Ferrer make it to La Paz, Bolivia, by train. There, at Argentinian Isaac Nogu's house, he meets other Argentinians, many of them anti-Peronist exiles. He becomes friends with a young lawyer named Ricardo Rojo.

Ernesto and Rojo share long ventures in Bolivia, where they do anthropological studies and get a hard look at the poverty and the rising despair.

At the time, Ernesto had no political background, but he did have insight. A flame started burning inside of him.

In Santiago, Cuba, Fidel and Raul Castro lead an assault on the Moncada barracks. It fails.

The Castro brothers led a rebel group against dictator Fulgencio Batista, a sergeant who had taken over the government in 1934 and led a "mock" coup in 1952 to prevent elections. At that time, Cuba was little more than a gigantic casino and brothel floating on the Caribbean for rich foreigners' entertainment—and for the Cuban people's misery.

33 rebels died in the Moncada assault. The Castro brothers and other revolutionaries were caught and judged in a court surrounded by soldiers. Fidel Castro, a 27 year-old lawyer, assumed his own defense and made a five-hour speech.

By the end of 1953, Ernesto Guevara and his friend Ricardo Rojo were in Costa Rica. They arrived there after a journey filled with accidents and adventures that took them through Columbia, Ecuador and Panama. They met other Argentinians and told them about their plans.

Guatemala was ruled by Jacobo Arbenz, a nationalist Colonel who was carrying out socialist reforms, like expropriating lárge landed estates of United Fruit, an American company that was manipulating Guatemala's economy.

Guevara and Rojo arrived in Guatemela in January 1954. As usual, they stayed at a cheap boarding house. They shared the place with several Peruvian exiles, on the run from Director Manuel Odría. In May, at the Organization of American States (OAS), the US Chancellor pitches Guatemala the ominous message:

From the south (Honduras, El Salvador and Nicaragua) troops are preparing an operation organized by the US State Department, the CIA and United Fruit...

In the meantime, Ricardo Rojo goes on to the States and Guevara stays behind in Guatemala, where his friendship to Hilda Gadea, a Peruvian refugee, grows more and more intense. They share a boarding house, archaeological outings, readings, political conversations...

At meetings with exiles from other Latin American countries, Ernesto entered more and more into the spirit of continental reality.

Once again President Arbenz gives proof of his gullibility.

On June 17, what everyone has been fearing occurs. Commanded by an insurgent Colonel—Carlos Castillo Armas—and with State Department, CIA and United Fruit support, lurking troops launch land and air raids on Arbenz's government.

As time passed, the situation worsened. Guevara felt the need to take action:

Despite his criticism, Ernesto felt as if Guatemala and its democracy were his own. He took to the streets to organize fighting groups among the workers. He attracted more attention than he'd bargained for...

So...

GUEVARA, GUEVARA, GET IN, FAST!
WHAT DO YOU WANT? WHO ARE YOU?
I'M NICASIO SANCHEZ TORAZO, AIDE AT THE EMBASSY. THERE'S NO TIME TO LOSE. COME WITH ME, MAN. THEY'RE OUT TO KILL YOU...
KILL ME? I ONLY WANT TO DEFEND...

At the Argentine Embassy, Guevara refuses to be repatriated. He gets a safe conduct pass for Mexico and sets out, with Hilda and the other refugees on a long train journey.

* Scornful term for Americans.

A dream of freedom

Mexico City is the capital of refugees: Guatemalans, Cubans, Peruvians, Dominicans, Nicaraguans, Spaniards running from Franco... all of them wind up there. Everybody dreams of going home and living in liberty. Ernesto is already somebody...

1955 was a year of important events:

* *Winston Churchill resigns as English Prime Minister, after having played a key role against Nazism and in beginning the Cold War, that pitted the Occidental Powers (USA, Great Britain, France, Germany) against the Communist bond.*

* *Albert Einstein dies. Winner of the Nobel Prize for Physics, he revolutionized modern physics with his Theory of Relativity, based on the principle that the passage of time is not the same for two observers moving in respect from one to another.*

* *Germany (except the Eastern part) regains its territorial sovereignty, that the Allied troops had occupied since the end of World War II.*

* *Juan Domingo Peron is defeated in Argentina on September 16, following a bloody coup d'état. General Eduardo Lonardi takes over, until General Pedro Eugenio Aramburu replaces him on November 13. Peronism is persecuted as it had previously done to its adversaries, and hostility deepens.*

On February 24 of that year, dictator Batista started a new government term in Cuba that he called "constitutional". Due to popular clamor, Fidel Castro and his brother Raul joined the rest of the exiles under an amnesty. At a Latin American refugee and rebel assembly, Hilda and Ernesto met Fidel, listened to his dreams and plans of freedom, his project to invade Cuba...

Guevara and Castro began meeting regularly and quickly became friends. Unaware, Mexico is providing the setting for a relationship that would shock the world.

As of the mid-1950s, 85% of Cuban farmers were not owners of their lands. Over 50% of the best farmlands belonged to United Fruit and West Indian (another American corporation). Over 3 million Cubans lacked electric light. Rickets and infant mortality decimated the population.

But Fidel had a plan.

Ernesto, already part of the group, wanted to oust Batista and all Latin American dictators: Dominican Trujillo, Venezuelan Péréz Jiménez, Colombian Rojas Pinilla, Haitian Duvalier, Paraguayan Stroessner, Nicaraguan Somoza...

* Cuban peasants

The rebel group was called Movimiento 26 de Julio* (in homage to Moncada). Soon it counted 80 men and 50 dollars donated by (rich and poor) Cuban refugees who believed in the need for social change. The rebels bought guns and started training as fighters on a borrowed piece of land, in Chalco.

* 26th of July Movement

Here Ernesto Guevara would show great solidarity with his peers, always aware of everyone's needs, even in the middle of a hard and demanding existence. This comes as no surprise to the Cubans who already know him.

Here, he also received his second baptism, the one in which he would be given the name that would enter history and legend.

He, age 27, was starting the decisive decade of his life. On February 15, 1956 a new circumstance entered his life. He wrote his parents at once.

Nine months later, after long hours of preparation and constant pressure from Batista's government, Fidel gathered his men and made an announcement:

On November 15, a small pleasure boat leisure ship called "Granma", waiving a red and black flag, left Tuxpan in the Gulf of Mexico. Its destiny, Santiago de Cuba.

The boat holds 20 men, but is carrying 82: Fidel Castro and his small army. Their armaments: rifles, ammunition and an immense will to change the history of their land.

The journey was supposed to last five days, but as the sea grew rough, the small boat could barely stay afloat. On December 2, it ran aground in Belic, a fishing village.

After making their way to the beach, the castaways start a long walk in search of the mountains. After three days on the exhausting march, they are battered. Che tries to soothe his comrades' blisters with the remains of his first aid kit.

There, the exhausted group was attacked by Batista's troops and Che received a new baptism: one of blood. He saw comrades dying and was wounded himself.

The few survivors split up into three groups and hid in the mountains for a week, without food.

Finally, the two tiny rebel groups come together. It's Fidel and his broth-r Raul, Camilo Cienfuegos, Che and a few more. They find out that only 2 others have survived the attack in which Crescencio Rodriguez led Batista's army against 100 revolutionaries.

Meanwhile, in Buenos Aires, Guevara's parents received a letter that he had sent them before boarding...

The 12 survivors hid from Batista's 30 thousand soldiers by climbing the mountains of the Sierra Maestra (a chain of mountains that is like the backbone of the island). They have a plan: to reorganize themselves, to start winning over the peasants' trust. Fidel gives a mandate:

With second-rate armament and exemplary discipline, enthusiasm and faith in their beliefs, the score of rebels start recruiting peasants fed up with poverty and injustice. On January 17, 1959 they gain their first victory, taking over a military post near the Magdalena river. On February 2, two months after disembarking, they come to Manzanillo, where a group of men recruited by the peasant Crescendio Sanchez joins them and Che receives something precious:

In those days, Che suffered from malaria attacks. Julio Zenon Acosta took care of him day and night until he recovered.

Acosta—who would die shortly after a battle—was Che's first student. Hereafter, he will have many more in Sierra Maestra. His life is in constant change: he's a doctor, a guerrilla, a teacher. They are all unified by one conviction:

In March, tropical rains, asthma and fatigue make him live the "worst days of the struggle in the Sierra". In those days he meets new revolutionaries that join the movement: Frank Pais, Haydé Santamaría, Vilma Espin, Hubert Matos, Celia Sanchez. The group gets bigger and branches out into three columns. He stays in the staff, with Fidel:

At every settlement the rebels reach, Che becomes the doctor of the peasants, who suffer from starvation, parasites, rickets, infections... He writes down his ideas and feelings.

On May 29, the Liberation Army (then 127 guerrillas strong) won its first resounding victory on assaulting the El Uvero quarter. Batista's troops lost 19 men, 14 were wounded, and another 14 were taken prisoner. Only 6 escaped. The rebels lost 6 men and 9 were wounded...but after that, no one in the world could ignore them.

Che fought with skill and valor. Afterwards, when his comrades had gone, he stayed behind to take care of the wounded. Years later, Fidel would recall: "He attends them, saves their lives and then rejoins the column along with them. He is indeed a capable and brave leader; one of those men that when there's a hard mission to do doesn't wait to be asked."

A few days later—after the engagement with the mass of the troops—a piece of news moves him. He is named Commander and Celia Sanchez pins the identity star on his beret.

In the first days of August 1957 Commander Che Guevara led his first action. He and his men attacked the Bueycito quarters, put the enemy to flight to the great delight of the people.

The rebels grew more numerous and strong. The people supported them increasingly. Batista answers back with blatant terrorism: Frank Pais is killed on the streets of Santiago.

The Dictator Batista gives the order to burn the peasants' huts. The young runaways go up into the mountains and join the rebels. The soldiers know better than to chase them there.

By the beginning of 1958, the rebels have become a real army. Commander Guevara is put in charge of building a field hospital. Some of his comrades and numerous peasants help him. A prestigious physician from La Habana donates an X Ray machine. Soon the hospital attends guerrillas, peasants, women, children. Che announces another initiative:

The stronger the Movimiento 26 de Julio grows and the weaker Batista's government becomes, the more those wanting to take advantage of the situation appear. In Miami several politicians without popular support (some of them ex-officials of corrupt administrations) sign a "Unity Agreement of Cuban Opposition to Batista's Dictatorship" that Castro and his men disavow.

In order to organize strikes, the Rebel Army sends support committees into the country and the cities. The revolutionary word runs through Cuba like an underground river. Then Che gets a new mission.

The peasants show their support by collecting reams of paper and liters of ink. With little more than an old typewriter and mimeograph machine, Che becomes editor of *El Cubano Libre*, the only free (not banned) people's newspaper in Cuba.

By this time, Commander Che Guevera's life was devoted entirely to his comrades, to the peasants, and to followers of the movement. His leadership was obvious—the other revolutionaries no longer mistook him for just another of the hundreds of rebels who grew more numerous every day. Che Guevera was a man who practiced what he preached; his everyday attitude served as an example for his comrades. He was a man who had overcome by force of will his own problematic health (he still suffered regular episodes of asthma, some so severe that they rendered him unconscious) to help his wounded comrades and to provide medical attention for the peasants. Che had his own way of maintaining inner strength: in his wife Hilda, Che had found a sensitive companion whose revolutionary dreams matched his own...and whenever he could, Che wrote—diaries, stories, poems...

The rebels began to get political support and arms from abroad, and they were respected and followed by increasing numbers of peasants and the people of the cities. On February 24, Rebel Radio began broadcasting from the Sierra Maestra and the Movimiento 26 de Julio began serving as a kind of parallel government.

While this was taking place, Che took charge of creating small primitive industries to supply food and clothing for the troops. He himself worked alongside the others.

On April 9 a general strike failed from lack of organization. On May 20 the government launched a brutal counterattack: 12 thousand Batista soldiers (supported by tanks and planes) marched against 300 guerrillas. Slaughter seemed certain.

...but two months later, the rebels—who moved around the Sierra like fish in water—had not only evaded the troops, but they gained the support of the peasants. The rebels touch-and-go tactics continued to befuddle and demoralize the army.

On July 20, 1958, a document was signed to unite all forces of the opposition backing the Movimiento 26 de Julio. The Communist Party—which considered Castro a well-intented adventurer—didn't go along with the pact. On August 21 Fidel called Camilo Cienfuegos and Che Guevara, his two top commanders:

Assigned Commander-in-Chief of all the Las Villas area, Che set out to accomplish his mission in charge of 170 men. For three months, they passed through storms, swamps and jungles, resisted enemy attacks, crossed towns, gained support, suffered hunger...

The two columns finally completed their missions. In Las Villas, Che, as commander, united all the small groups that were already fighting against Batista, making them leave sectarian interests behind. To get final support from the provincial peasantry he makes a startling announcement:

As 1958 came to an end, the Cuban revolutionaries controlled more and more territory, and gain increasing popularity in their country and throughout the world. In the previous two years, some transcendental events had taken place in Argentina and in other parts of the world:

In Latin America, Colombian dictator Rojas Pinilla (in 1957) and the Venezuelan Pérez Jiménez (in 1958) fell. In Cuba and the continent Batista's discredit grows. In Las Villas, after Che managed to unify all the rebel groups, the revolutionary command made a decision.

By that time, there were five revolution newspapers and several radio stations, so the word spread quickly. As before, Che and Camilo were put in charge of the two columns, enlarged with new recruits. The combat is now frontal (not guerrilla hit-and-run). Upon taking Sancti Spíritu, Che issued an edict.

After several consecutive victories, Che and Camilo moved their columns on to Santa Clara. Che and his men started the operation on December 29 at 5 in the morning. They took the University, Loma del Capiro and the Public Works building. Batista's army officers fled, his men surrendered or were put to flight. A train carrying arms and reinforcements arrived. The rebels assaulted it and took possession.

At noon, Che and his men attacked the city—astonishingly, the people helped them. They came out onto the streets carrying whatever they could get their hands on and blocked the way of the enemy tanks. From the house roofs, they threw gasoline and oil down on Batista's soldiers.

On the 1st of January 1959, Che ordered the final attack on the police headquarters, where the enemy staff was taking refuge.

In the midst of this battle came the news that the revolutionaries have been dreaming of for years:

And while some of Batista's soldiers ran and others surrendered, the city and the rebels that freed it celebrated.

That night the two commanders received an order from Fidel: **advance on La Habana** (Havana). On the dawn of January 2, Che and Camilo set out for the capital to make certain that none of the advantage-takers "appropriate" the revolution.

Rebel Radio carries Fidel's voice all over the country.

On the 14th of July La Habana welcomes Che and Camilo with massive popular demonstrations.

On the 6th of January, Fidel entered on La Habana. The Revolution had finally been won. After years of not being the master of its destiny, Cuba begins an era of profound change, hard battles, demanding realities.

In the heart of history

As the Revolutionary Government got under way, Che Guevara occupied a special place in the heart of the Cubans.

The revolutionaries had succeeded. Their dreams of a free Cuba were finally a reality. Now Cuba must face her own problems, which, in a sense, had just begun...

Cuba is the largest island in the Caribbean. Occupying about 42 thousand square miles, it looks like a sleeping alligator. Cuba was "discovered" by Christopher Columbus on October 27, 1492. In 1959, the newly freed Cuba had some 8 million inhabitants, two-thirds of whom were considered white, the other third, black or mixed. For most of its post-Columbus life, Cuba's main source of wealth was from sugar and nickel. In the 16th century, Cuba was the main commercial hub of the Americas. It's territory was fought over by Spain and the U.S. In 1898, on signing the Treaty of Paris, Cuba gained a relative autonomy, in which the U.S. was allowed to intervene to "preserve" life, freedom, and property and to "sustain" an "adequate" government. (SuperPowers speak with Forked Tongue.)

Throughout Cuba's history, patriots would always have to fight hard against those who claimed their domain. After declaring independence in 1869, Cuba loses it on being invaded by Spain and then by the United States, which attacked the Spanish forces and defeated them. The writer and revolutionary José Martí was the main hero of these struggles. He founded the Cuban Revolutionary Party in 1892, started an insurrection in 1895 and died in combat on May 19.

Until 1959 Cuba showed little of her history's splendors. She was an impoverished island known for her casinos and brothels until her disregarded people demanded urgent social changes.

Che spent many hours in this new stage of his life passionately studying Cuban history. He realized that it was a prerequisite for achieving real independence.

The idea of giving the revolution a socialist bearing developed in conversations with Fidel and Raul Castro. Though they distrust the Communists and Lenin's (soviet leader who headed the Russian Revolution) ideas, they think it is the best way for social change.

In the U.S. some sectors are starting to become wary of the new situation in Cuba.

EL MUNDO

Pressures on Cuba are demanded so that US interests may not be affected

On January 21, in front a multitude, Fidel gives a warning:

On February 9 of 1959, a decree formally communicates a decision that Fidel himself had already told Che about a few days before.

Ernesto Guevara, Che, is now "a Cuban native, with all rights and obligations." Che wastes no time in making two announcements:

Che becomes obsessed with the notion of industrializing Cuba. He wants to rescue Cuba from the setback that her exclusive dependence on sugar (and tobacco) has sentenced her to. He dedicates long hours of study in order to understand the situation, talk sense and plan a different future.

Through his studies, he learns that 40% of the Cuban workers live in the countryside. They are the poor, hardened, battered men and women he has met during the guerrilla campaign. And their offspring are the children who suffer malnutrition, diseases and premature deaths.

After studying reports from international economic organizations, economy surveys and specialized authors, he came to a more firm conclusion.

When a staff of economists prepare a ten-year plan for development, Che bursts out:

At the Revolution's staff meetings his stand grows increasingly vigorous.

But before moving on, the Revolution has to sort out certain matters. There are two lines of thinking. One, moderate that doesn't want profound changes, is headed by President Manuel Urrutia—a lawyer who defended Fidel when he was charged—the other by Fidel (Prime Minister) and the fighters of the Sierra Maestra. The dispute intensifies as the need to take urgent measures increases.

Meanwhile, some changes have also occurred in Che's private life. His wife and daughter are in Mexico, his marriage is falling apart, and his relation with Aleida March, his guerrilla comrade and current assistant, grows more and more passionate...

Intensive work without rest weakens him and he suffers a severe asthmatic crisis. During his recuperation in March of 1959, he writes a letter to the Revolution newspaper:

Fidel still believes that the US will support the Revolution even though it has affected big private American interests. He goes and talks in Washington and New York.

From Buenos Aires, where he was attending a Latin American economic conference, Fidel proposes a plan:

In May of 1959 the Agrarian Reform Law is proclaimed. All lots larger than 990 acres will be distributed among the landless peasant cooperatives. Landholders with estates up to this size may keep their lands as long as they work them themselves.

All the suspicion that "the bearded ones" had aroused in the US—which did not have a realistic understanding of Latin America—breaks out here and now:

In the Cuban government, Urrutia's moderate sector expresses fears that ties with the US may break. Fidel takes a stand:

Che has already become Fidel's main adviser. In June he writes two articles for the Brazilian magazine *O Cruzeiro* where he describes how he met Fidel, how he joined the Revolution and how they became the best of friends.

By the time Che marries Aleida March on June 2, the Revolution is under constant attack from the US and its allies and is left with only one option: to look for new allies. Che takes a definite stand:

While Guevara is on his mission, a government crisis comes to an end when president Urrutia is replaced by Osvaldo Dorticós Torrado. Che meets with Nasser in Egypt, with Tito in Yugoslavia, with Nehru in India, with Sukarno in Indonesia. His reputation spreads throughout the world.

Excited and full of conviction, he comes back from his tour in September. What he has seen, heard and experienced convinces him of the steps to be taken.

Meanwhile in Cuba profound revolutionary steps have been taken. Dozens of buildings are turned into schools; voluntary teachers lists are opened. This is paid for with liquor taxes. The government of the young rebels—33 is the average age—begins to make collective dreams come true.

Most of the people are thrilled in spite of the growing American hostility, but some ex-guerrillas oppose the radical changes. Hubert Matos, among them, rebels against Fidel. Along with his followers, he is judged and condemned to prison. US pirate planes bomb and burn cane fields.

When an airplane in which Camilo Cienfuegos was traveling disappears, Fidel loses one of his three most reliable men (the others being his brother Raul and Che). Che is the most radical of the revolutionaries.

* In Spanish, a term meaning foreigners, especially Americans

Being neutral meant abstaining from the control game between the two great Powers that were engaged in the Cold War: the US and the USSR. In 1959, the US proclaims that Latin America is its area of influence and there can be no neutral countries in that region. The tension with General Dwight Eisenhower's government grows, but this does not stop Cuba's projects for industrialization and independence. On October 7 of 1959, after Che lays out a series of plans for development he has been working on, Fidel announces:

Shortly after Che's announcement—on November 26, 1959—he is named Chairman of the National Bank of Cuba, in place of economist Felipe Pazos, making Che the head of the Cuban economy. It's a hard job: the US is pressing more and more. Threatening not to buy any sugar, it impedes other countries (Great Britain and Belgium) from selling Cuba planes and arms. These attitudes reinforce the Cuban's patriotic feeling and the decision to defend the process they are living.

Guevera so perfectly exemplified the people and their Revolution, that when new currency was issued, Che's image appeared on bills and coins as a symbol of The New Man.

He worked in his office from hoon to 3 in the morning, studies, decides measures, has mate, smokes a pipe and always dresses as if he were in broad combat in the Sierra. On December 26 of 1959 he produces his first bank report:

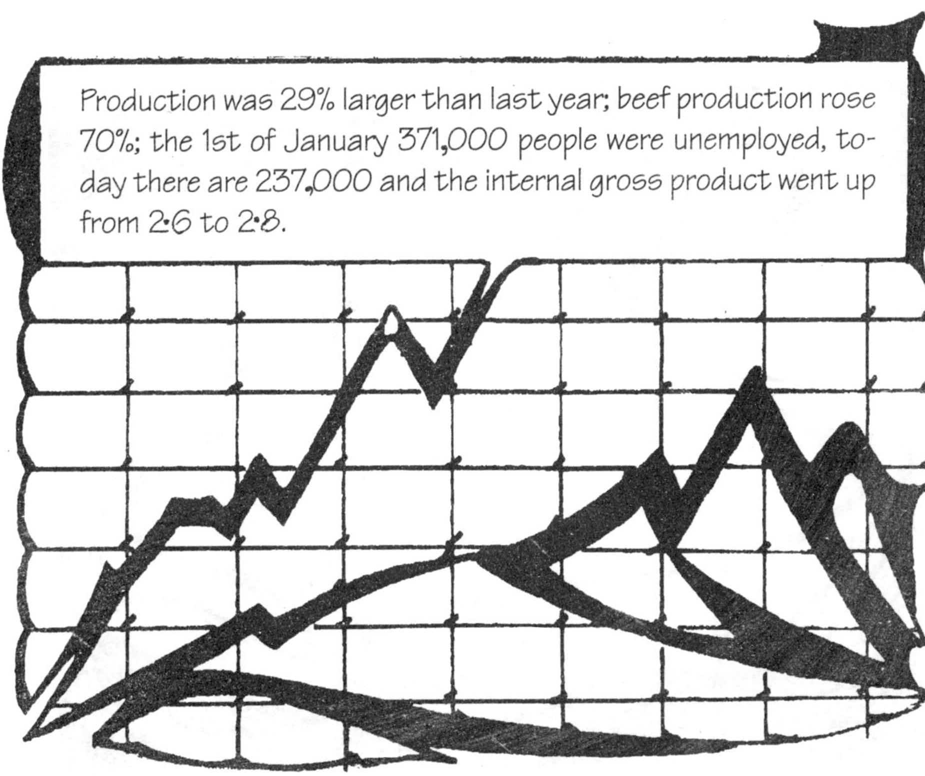

From his post Che dictated controls on luxury imports, imposing high taxes on them, while at the People Stores the stock of primary necessity goods increased. He answered the criticism of some sectors through an interview.

Among his initiatives was the great increase in sugar trade (from 1 million tons to 1 million 900 thousand), which brings him closer to one of his dreams: speeding the industrialization.

Amazingly, he even finds the time to write and publish a book—*The War of Guerrillas*—that he dedicates to Camilo Cienfuegos and in which he expresses his ideas, his experiences, his reflection on what he's lived through and learned. He defines the essence of the guerrilla in three points:

Along with establishing the Theory of the Focus (that years later urban guerrilla groups would misunderstand and mistake for Messianism), the book contains his profile of the guerrilla:

All eyes were on Cuba. The military of the US Pentagon and the Latin American countries had studied Che's book in the hope of countering revolutions. In February 1960, the Soviet Minister Anastas Mikoyan visited Cuba and offered economic aid, even though the Revolution didn't follow soviet orthodoxy. Shortly after Mikoyan's visit, French existentialist philosopher Jean Paul Sartre and his companion, writer Simone de Beauvoir visited Cuba. After his visit, Sartre came to some interesting conclusions:

The Cold War was at a critical stage, relations between the US and the USSR were getting worse all the time for political, economical and strategic reasons. Che, then doing a lot of talking with marxist economist Carlos Rafael Rodríguez, launched a fast industrialization plan in May, in an attempt to produce many products other than sugar. These steps worried the US to the point that they threatened to buy no more sugar and sell no more fuel. Che became the public spokesman for Cuba's industrialization.

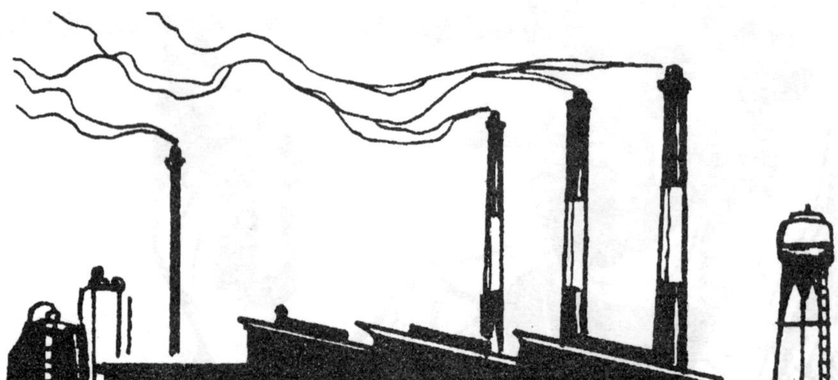

In the eyes of the Americans, he became the focus of suspicion. On August 8 of 1960, he was on the cover of *Time* magazine—they called him "a fascinating and dangerous figure".

The US stopped buying Cuban sugar, but was soon replaced by the USSR and China. Che decided that no more debts were to be paid. In September a massive popular assembly (hundreds of thousands people attend) approved a repudiation—written by Fidel, Raul and Che—on the American intervention. The US replied by suspending all trade with Cuba.

Che was quickly becoming the most solid ideologist of the Cuban Revolution. He published an essay ("Notes for the Study of Cuban Revolution Ideology") in which he wrote: "The Cuban revolution takes up Marx where he put down the science to take up a revolutionist's gun. It does so not out of a revisionist spirit, nor to revive the pure Marx, but simply because Marx, the scientist, set aside History and the past to study and predict the future. We, the practical revolutionaries...are simply conforming to the scientific Marx's predictions. The Marxist laws are present in the events of the Cuban Revolution, regardless of whether or not Cuba's leaders know these laws well from a theoretical point of view."

In November of 1960 John Fitzgerald Kennedy—a democrat—was elected president of the United States. Hopes of a "peaceful coexistence" between the two big Powers unravelled, a fact that might benefit Cuba. *Time* magazine published an interview with Che:

Che was already the most influential man in Cuba after Fidel. His "resume" shows more and more facets. Historian Hubert Mathews defined Guevara this way:

"He is no dogmatist. I never met anyone who personifies the rebel as amazingly as the Argentinian Ernesto Guevara. He rebels instinctively against society, country, Church and all institutions (...)
He is the most intelligent of all encircling Fidel and possesses the non-Cuban characteristic of being well organized in his work."

Books and newspaper articles with revolutionary war reports began to appear everywhere. Che urged the press and writers to respect the truth in their narrative, not to exaggerate or glorify in vain. A Cuban journalist friend of his got a letter from Guevara:

Celia, his mother, visited him in Cuba and was enraptured with the revolution that her beloved son helped set in motion. She published a series of stories on the revolution in the socialist paper *La Vanguardia*, edited by Alicia Moreau de Justo in Buenos Aires.

She wrote: *"The guerrillas have learned to fight, fighting and to govern, governing. Each one has discovered in himself unsuspected conditions that emerged from the sleeping bottom of his personality and made him capable of carrying out the most diverse works."*

On February 5, 1961, the legendary Argentinian socialist leader Alfredo L. Palacios—an unconditional admirer of the new Cuba—was elected deputy, thanks to the support of the youth, who admire the revolution Palacios praised. Che enjoyed the triumph at a distance. In turn, he admired Palacios, whom he had met a few months before In Cuba.

Another distinguished Argentinian, philosopher Ezequiel Martínez Estrada (author of the fundamental Xray of the Pampa) visited Cuba at the time, not only to get acquainted with the surprising and original revolution, but with "that legendary Argentinian", Che, as well. Writes Martínez Estrada:

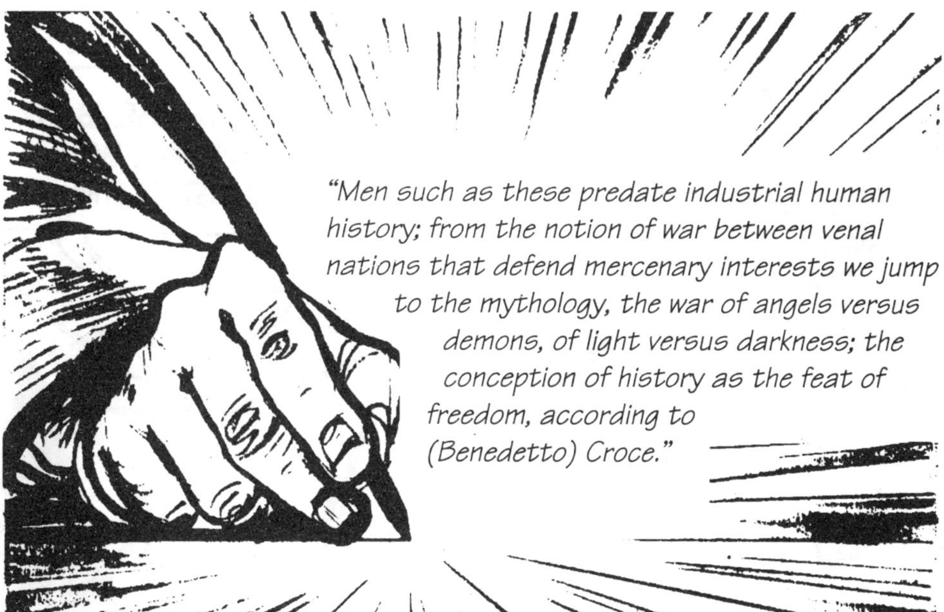

In long nights of mate tea and conversation, Martínez Estrada and Che discuss public and private matters. They develop a profound friendship. After the farewell, the philosopher recalls: " He who could be my son, paternally takes me by the arm as if he should accomplish with me his mission to protect and to guide".

Meanwhile, Cuba is having a hard time. Three days before leaving office, in January 1961, Eisenhower breaks relations with La Habana. The new American government continues preparing an invasion that the former had started to plan. The chief of the CIA (Central Intelligence Agency) sells Kennedy on a false notion:

On the 17th of April, 1961 the invasion took place, immediately resulting in a disgraceful defeat of the anti-Castrists. They were defeated by the 250 thousand soldiers of the Rebel Army, whose training was under Che's charge. The Cuban patriots used arms and planes supplied by the USSR and Czechoslovakia. Playa Girón, in Bahía Cochinos*, became a historical landmark: the Cuban Revolution won its first battle against an invader. In turn, Kennedy's government suffered its first big crisis. The president did not try to pass the buck...

* Girón Beach, Cochinos Bay

On the 1st of May, Workers Day, there was a gigantic rally in La Habana. Homage was paid to the Playa Girón heroes who defeated the gusanos* (this is what anti-Castrists are called). Then Fidel made a transcendental announcement:

Shortly after, this is added to the initiative of founding the Socialist Revolution of Cuba Unique Party (PURSC)**, wherein the 26th of July Movement (pro-Fidel), the Revolutionary Directory (students) and the Popular Socialist Party (communist) unite. The communists try to take hold of the command. This is avoided thanks to Che's initiative.

* Gusanos: Spanish for worms.

** Partido Unico de la Revolución Socialista de Cuba

On June 3 in Vienna, Kennedy met with Nikita Khrushchev, the Soviet president. Khrushchev gave a warning:

At the time a group of students visited Che at the Ministry of Industry. They wanted to pay him homage for Playa Girón. They were met with an exemplary answer.

On August 5 of 1961, economic ministers from all America gathered in Punta del Este, Uruguay. They intended to design the Alliance for Progress, a continental economy aid plan financed by the US. Fidel sent Che as Cuban representative. When he arrived at the Carrasco airport, in Montevideo, thousands of people were waiting for him.

Hundreds of Argentinians journeyed to Punta del Este to greet their legendary fellow countryman. Che's parents were there, along with his brothers and sisters and several dear old friends.

Che's eagerly awaited speech was not given until the third day of the conference. He spoke on Thursday 8, after Argentinian Raúl Presbisch, representative of SEPAL (UN Special Commission for Latin America) who strongly criticized the directives that the International Monetary Fund (IMF) intended to impose. Che spoke straight to the point:

OURS IS AN AGRARIAN, ANTI-FEUDAL, ANTI-IMPERIALISTIC REVOLUTION THAT HAS GRADUALLY TURNED INTO A SOCIALIST REVOLUTION DUE TO INTERNAL EVOLUTION AND EXTERNAL ATTACKS. SO WE PROCLAIM IT: A SOCIALIST REVOLUTION!

WE WANT THEM TO LET US BE, TO LET US GROW, SO THAT WITHIN 20 YEARS WE MAY ALL MEET AGAIN TO SEE IF THE SONG OF THE SIREN WAS THAT OF REVOLUTIONARY CUBA OR OF SOME OTHER.

WE CANNOT HELP EXPORTING OUR EXAMPLE, BECAUSE EXAMPLE IS SOMETHING SPIRITUAL THAT GOES BEYOND THE BOUNDARIES.

The Alliance for Progress allocated 20 billion dollars to Latin-American development, excepting Cuba (due to American pressure). In spite of this, the possibility of a compromise between the US and Cuba (that would not come about) is negotiated within a month. At the time Che is the favorite target of journalists from all over the world, giving two answers that portray him in his full dimension:

The meeting ends on the 16th and Che holds several conferences before Uruguayan students and workers. Then, on August 18, he travels secretly to Buenos Aires to meet with president Arturo Frondizi. The meeting takes place without the knowledge of Argentina's military—because they would have opposed it. Che returns to Uruguay immediately and goes on to Brazil, where he is received by president Janio Quadros. Both presidents were trying to make their countries grow through development (Frondizi) and reform (Quadros) plans. They both wanted to mediate between the US and Cuba. They were both overthrown by their countries' military (Frondizi in March 1962, Quadros on the same August of 1961, after receiving the Che). Many years later, the Argentine president would remember Guevara in this way:

The world situation grew increasingly tense (on August 16 of 1961, Berlin is split in two when Communist authorities raise the Wall). In Cuba, the economic situation began to suffer from the U.S. blockade. Che admits mistakes on his part: he realizes that enthusiasm and passion are not enough to maintain the production level. Fidel Castro declares the Revolution as Marxist and by the end of January 1962 Kennedy gets Cuba expelled from the OAS (Organization of American States). Cuba votes against the proposal. Argentina, Mexico, Brazil, Bolivia, Chile and Ecuador abstain.

The most conservative US sectors and the Anti-Castro refugees ask Kennedy's government to take more severe measures. Bases of soviet nuclear missiles are set up on Cuban territory to defend it from a new (and possible) invasion. American spy planes discover them.

The crisis erupts in October. American Pentagon military want to bomb Cuba, even at the risk of unleashing a nuclear war. Kennedy manages to convince them of first trying a total blockade. Distress envelops the world: the war between the US and the USSR seems inevitable!

On October 27, the crisis comes to an end. The USSR agrees to remove the missiles under UN supervision, and the US, in turn, signs a pact of non-aggression on Cuba. Che, who occupies a military post in Pinar del Río during the crisis, does not agree with the solution, but obeys it.

At the time, as Minister of Industry, Che admits a mistake: you cannot industrialize Cuba in haste at the expense of the agriculture. Victim of years of underdevelopment, the country has to go on being a crop exporter, mainly sugar.

The Cuban Revolution becomes the USSR's main debtor, to Che's distress, since he had dreamt of an autonomous debt-free Cuba. Set to intensify agricultural production Guevara finds himself in another controversy with the communists. They believe in material motivations to the workers, whereas Che supports the importance of moral motivations.

Che becomes more and more the leader of Cuban autonomy. He opposes the growing communist interference in the Revolution, that is now nearly three years old.

Che proclaims that the Cubans should face the production and the work in the same spirit as they faced the combat. In his letters, he defends the Cuban right to make their own "wild and joyous" revolution. And he starts signing his letters with a slogan that the government soon adopts for all its statements and documents.

Before his closest comrades, he defines his idea of Socialism:

He also fights against the least sign of privilege. At every factory he visits he reminds the workers that their dedication is needed for their children to receive the fruits of the Revolution. To set an example, he himself went to the cane fields to cut sugarcane.

In the little free time he has, he writes *The War of Guerrillas: a method.* With that book he intended to send a message to the Latin American countries. It was also a message for the US: excluded from the Latin American community, Cuba feels free to export her model.

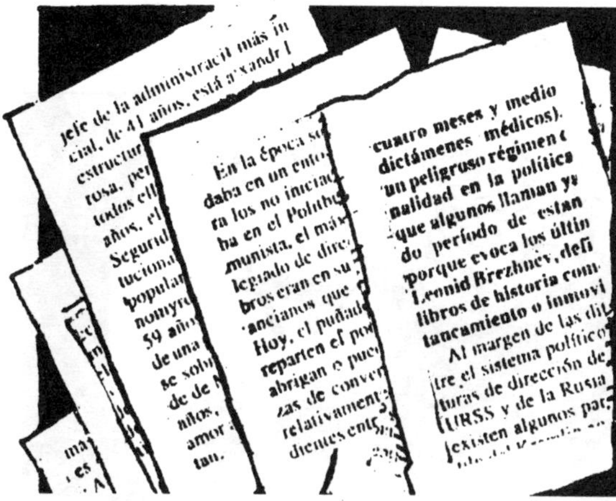

Our duty is to be sensitive before all world exploitation and injustices. **Martí** said: *"Every true man should feel on the cheek the blow to another man's".*

Among his proposals of that time, there is one to transform the "were-wolf" of capitalist society into a New Man. In that hard year of 1963, two key men of the century vanish from scene....

On the 3rd of June, the great humanist who updated the Church and fought for social justice, **Pope John 23rd**, dies in Rome....

On November 22, president **Kennedy** is assassinated in Dallas and the crime is attributed to ultra-conservative forces of the American establishment.

Vice-president Lyndon Johnson—a tough texan—becomes the new president of the US. He immerses his country in the Vitnam War, the great American defeat of the century. The North Vietnamese victory will occur nine years later and be considered as a vindication of the whole Third World. Meanwhile, in 1964, Che assumes the voice of Cuba in several international forums—especially economical—and attacks unconditionally the US intervention policy.

On March 31,1964, a military coup installs a dictatorship (headed by General Humberto Castelo Branco) in Brazil. That terrorist government will last for more than two decades. Brazil breaks relations with Cuba, as Argentina had done shortly after Frondizi's overthrow. The army pressures president Arturo Umberto Illia so that he will not resume relations with Cuba. In October, the OAS decides that all its countries break relations with Cuba. Only Mexico disobeys. Che, in front of a French journalist, does not silence his ideas.

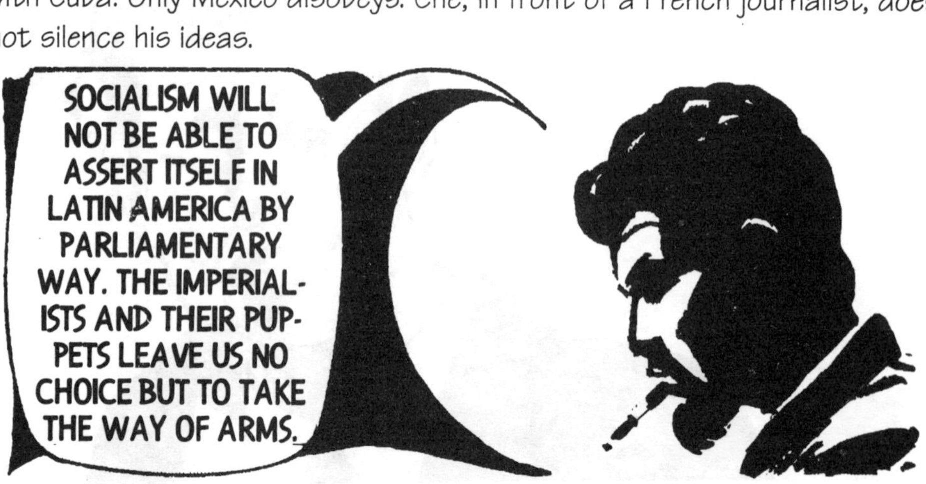

On 27 May 1964, Indian prime minister, peace and independence leader of the Third World, Sri Pandit Jawaharlal Nehru dies. On 15 July Nikita Khrushchev is removed from power in the USSR and replaced by conservative Leonid Brezhnev. The worldwide panorama becomes increasingly warlike. In Cuba, Che's stature weakens on account of his economic misstep of neglecting the sugar production for a quick—and unsuccessful—industrialization. Still he remains morally and ideologically invulnerable and his ideas keep coming out in the letters, documents and texts he writes continuously.

During that time, school compositions from Cuban children were handed on to Che, touching him to realize some aspects of his own life.

In domestic politics, he fights fiercely for his ideas. He is considered a hard-core: he thinks collective efforts and compromise should be redoubled, he rejects material motivations. The soft one is the president Dorticós (supported by the old communist guard), who propounds material stimulus and certain forms of rent and individual profit. Fidel has to act as arbiter. The USSR presses against Che's proposals.

The idea, once set in his mind, begins growing there. His opinions become freer and more radical.

On December 11 of 1964, Che speaks at the UN General Assembly. He attacks the US intervention policy with strength and irony. When the American representative accuses him of being a communist, he defends himself with brilliance and fiery words and ends with a premonitory phrase:

He takes advantage of being at the UN Assembly by making contact with the delegations of African countries. He is invited to Ghana, Guinea and Mali. He goes to Africa immediately. He spreads his ideas about the New Man, about the necessity of pressing the USSR so that they support the decolonization processes not only with words, but economically. (The USSR declines.) Africans call him 'The Mao of Latin America,' remembering Chinese leader Mao Tse Tung and his theory of permanent revolution.

After participating in February in a neutral country meeting in Algeria, he travels incognito to China and meets with Mao. He commits himself to lead armed rebellions throughout the continent to extend the revolution and asks China for the help. Mao agrees on the condition that Che stay in Cuba to counteract the Soviet influence.

Guevara refuses to be used as a pawn in the political maneuvering between China and the USSR. He sees it as a new obstacle to his dream of extending the revolutionary example all over the Americas. His frustration provokes a severe asthma attack that leads to a heart condition. Chinese doctors save his life miraculously.

He returns to Cuba, in March of 1964, after three months abroad. He finds Fidel so harassed by the Cuban communists that he had bowed under the USSR's wing, in exchange for economic help. More than ever Che believes that the allies should be other Latin-American countries. He has a long secret conversation with Castro. He feels very much alone in the Cuban government's panorama. He needs new roads to travel.

Immediately, Che goes on a retreat to meditate and plan his strategy. He goes to a cane field with his friend Alberto Granados. From there, he decides to go back to the life of a guerrilla—but first, he writes his parents a letter. His mother will not get to read it. Celia de la Serna dies in May of 1965 without knowing Ernestito, her youngest grandson.

Dear folks:

...I'm back on the road with my shield in arm...
I must live in accordance with my beliefs...
many may say I'm an adventurer and I am, but one of a different kind, one who puts his life on the line to prove his truths...
I've loved you greatly, but that I have not known how to to express my love...
my will shall sustain my flaccid legs and my weary lungs...
remember this little condottiero of the 20th century...*
A bear hug from your prodigal and recalcitrant son...

Ernesto

* Conductor in Italian

The plan is complete. It's time for goodbyes. Che sends letters to the people he loves most. Each one carries his feelings, his thoughts, his outlook on life. To his companion of juvenile adventures, Alberto Granados, he writes:

"I don't know what to leave you. So I oblige you to go into the economy and sugar cane. My dreams shall have no limits until the bullets say so...I expect you, sedentary gypsy, when the smell of gun-fire abates."

Among all the letters one stands out: it's for **Fidel.**

"I have fulfilled the part of my duty that tied me to the Revolution in this territory and I say goodbye to you, to my comrades, to this land that is already mine...I formally resign to my charges....other lands of the world demand my modest efforts...the time has come for us to separate...I do so with a mixture of joy and pain...here I leave the purest of my hopes..."

"...If the final hour should meet me under other skies my last thought shall be for these people and for you... I leave my wife and my children nothing material and it grieves me not; I'm glad that it be so...Till Victory Forever...Country or Death! Embracing you with full revolutionary fervor: CHE."

Just before Che's life would slowly begin to fuse into mystery and legend, on March 12 of 1965, the weekly paper *Marcha*, of Montevideo published Guevara's fundamental texts; parts of it:

Socialism and man in Cuba

* The faults of the past move to the present in the individual conscience and it is necessary to work continually to eradicate them.

* The new society has to compete very strongly with the past.

* On the personal conscience weighs the debris of an education aimed at isolating the individual. To build socialism, simultaneously with the material foundation the "new man" has to be made.

* The instrument of change should essentially be of a moral kind, without forgetting a correct use of material motivations, above all of social nature.

* In socialism, in spite of its apparent standardization, man is more whole; in spite of that, his chance of expressing himself and making himself felt in the social system is infinitely greater.

* The shift does not come about automatically in the conscience, as it does not in the economy either. Variations are slow and not rhythmical; there are periods of acceleration; others of pause, and even of regression.

* Our vanguard revolutionaries must idealize their love for the people.

* It is necessary to have a great dose of humanity, a great dose of sense of justice and of truth, so as not to fall into dogmatic extremes, into cold scholasticisms, in isolation of the masses.

* Each day it is necessary to fight because this love for living mankind must be transformed into concrete facts, into actions that may serve for example, for mobilization.

* Our children must have and lack whatever the common man has and lacks; our family must understand this and fight for it. The revolution is done through man, but man has to forge day by day his revolutionary spirit.

On the way to legend

On October 3 of 1965, Fidel officially said goodbye to Che, after reading in public the letter Che left him. This puts to rest the rumors that the Cuban communists had killed Guevara. From then on the Cuban government's pro-Soviet sectors gained more and more power: Che departed for Africa. He arrived at Brazaville (ex-French Congo) along with a small group of Cuban guerrillas. From there he planned to join in the struggle of the ex-Belgian Congo's rebels against Moisé Tshombé, the colonialist president.

In March of 1966, Che left Africa with the hundred men that had accompanied him. Fidel has asked him to do so ("the Cuban presence there compromises Revolution"). Castro wanted him in Cuba, where the First Solidarity Conference of the People of Asia, Africa and Latin America (the Tricontinental) was meeting, with 450 participants. But Che prefers to continue on his way toward South America. Che wears a disguise so that he can travel incognito around Uruguay, Brazil and Paraguay to get into the spirit of the social and political situation.

On June 28 of 1966, president Arturo Ilia is overthrown in Buenos Aires and General Juan Carlos Onganía usurps power. A few weeks later, he orders the police to destroy the University on the tenebrous "Night of the long sticks". People are wounded and arrested and many professors and students go into exile. The conditions are beginning to set the stage for what ten years later would lead to "the Process", one of the greatest contemporaneous genocides (30,000 people will be missing and killed), started by General Videla, Admiral Massera and Brigadier Agosti; it will last seven years under the command of other military leaders.

For Che, Onganía's subversive coup had brought about the conditions for setting up a guerrilla focus in Argentina. He arrived in Córdoba with his disguise and stays twenty days with the intention of recruiting young guerrillas. No luck. His new destination is Bolivia: he enters with a new face and becomes Adolfo .Mena, "special envoy from the Organization of American States", who has come to study the economic and social conditions that prevail in the Bolivian scene. On September 3 of 1966 the Bolivian government formally receives him and offers him all the necessary cooperation.

There he meets with the Roberto (Coco) and Guido (Inti) Peredo brothers, Bolivians he met in 1965, at La Habana. They think it is possible to create a rebel focus in Bolivia. Together, they design a strategy.

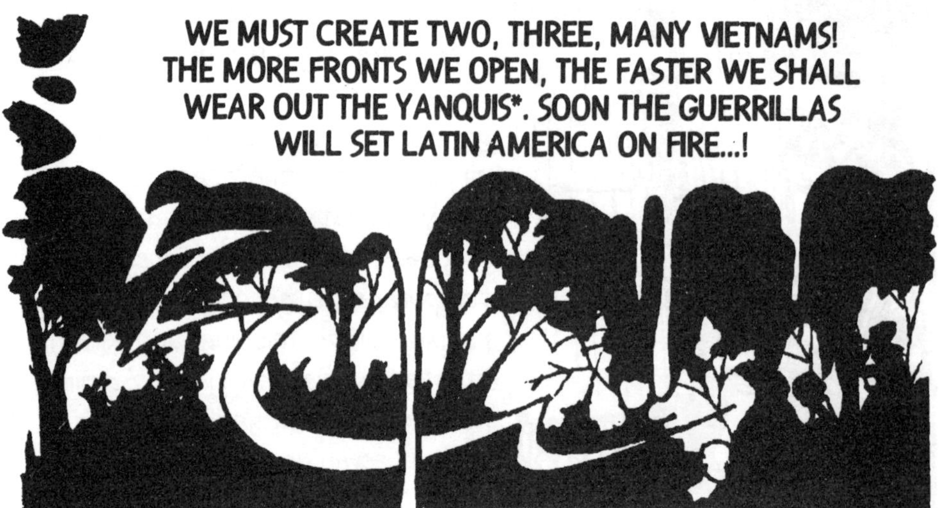

* Descriptive term for Americans

At the Ñiancahuazú Canyon, in southern Bolivia, 63 miles from the end of the river Grande, which divides the country in two, the first guerrilla operation base is set up. In the following months more Cuban fighters arrive and Bolivian guerrillas are recruited in the area, from both the countryside and the University.

The area is inhabited by leopards, wild boars, and every variety of insects. On November of 1966 the group is consolidated. By Christmas Eve, Che has already begun writing his Campaign Diary and is already called Ramón, his nom de guerre. He and his fighters prepare a modest Christmas celebration and toast "to the success of the enterprise".

A few days later he is taken aback by the Bolivian Communist Party's disclosure (through its highest officer, Mario Monje) that they intend to control the movement and reduce its aggressiveness so as to not compromise the USSR.

Che's idea is to dominate the Nñancahuazú area and move forward from there in small groups, gaining the support of the peasantry (exploited by general Barrientos' dictatorship), on to Cochabamba (west) and Santa Cruz (south). True to his theory, he intends to continue creating rebel forces.

Marcos, a Cuban, is named chief of the vanguard group, that is going onward to Vallegrande. Other names that will form part of the legend are already in the guerrilla army: the Argentinians Ciro Bustos and Laura Gutiérrez Bauer (Tania), the Peruvian Capac, El Chino, Mogambo, Tuma, Pombo, the Cuban doctor Moro and Regis Debray, a French professor of philosophy, 26, who goes by the nom de guerre Dantón and whom Che, in his Diary, would call a "good intellectual and lousy guerrilla". The contingent prepares shelters and combat supplies.

On February 26, while they are making their way through the jungle, the group suffers what Che calls "our baptism of death". A guerrilla called Rolando stumbles and falls into the Grande River and drowns. Several backpacks and another man are lost in a new accident. Some of the men start feeling depressed and discouraged. Shall the enterprise succeed or is it a quixotic action?

The 27th of March of 1967 is—writes Che—"a day of warlike events". It's the first confrontation with the Bolivian army, after ambushing a patrol that, suspecting something, had gone into the jungle. Seven soldiers die, 14 are taken prisoner, 4 are wounded, armament is captured. After this, 2000 men start surrounding the area and preparing planes and napalm to throw there.

The guerrilla war specializes in hit-and-run. Che knows the actions have started sooner than what was foreseen (his plan was to start in September of 1967). Now there is in no turning back. Four men are expelled from the guerrilla force since their loyalty is suspect. Another 13 desert for fear of confrontation with the rangers (military trained by Americans). The rebels divide in two groups: 25 in one commanded by Che, 17 in the other headed by Joaquín. On April 3 they march on to Vallegrande. The army, under the command of general Ovando Candia, arrives at the abandoned camp shortly after the rebels have evacuated it.

On April 11 in Iripití, a bloody combat takes place. Eleven soldiers die, seven rebels are killed. Until that day the guerrillas have suffered only one casualty in combat—Rubio, a Cuban guerrilla. He is buried in the jungle while Che writes in his Diary: "No Bolivian peasant has joined us yet... it is a key factor to solve".

On April 21, after long deliberation, Debray and Bustos leave the guerrillas. They embark on a mission to spread the word among the Bolivian people. However, they are soon captured in Yacunday. In his diary Che does not fool himself: "We are becoming more and more isolated; there is neither discipline nor resourcefulness. Much remains to be done so as to turn this into a fighting force, though the morale is high".

Little by little, more ranger divisions, green berets (US troops defeated in the Vietnam War) and planes start joining in the fight against the National Liberation Army (this is how the guerrillas have named themselves). The peasants, demobilized, do not join the guerrillas.

On May 15 of 1967, the rebels attack a train that connects Santa Cruz de la Sierra to Yacuiba and take hold of 50 tons of army food supplies. At the same time Che's column confronts an army patrol at the Grande river. Seven soldiers and two guerrillas are killed.

On June 24, on the night of San Juan, martial law is declared and army troops occupy the Huanuni, Cataví and Siglo XX mines. In the operation 24 miners are killed, among them women and children, and 72 are wounded.

Che and the guerrillas roam through the jungle avoiding frontal encounters. They are frustrated because of peasant indifference. "They're impenetrable as rocks"—Che writes in his Diary. After several combats, capturing a town (Samaipata), inflicting numerous casualties on the army and suffering losses (among them that of Inti Peredo), Che writes:

On August 31 a battalion of 30 men from the Bolivian army—acting on information from a cowardly peasant who had sold food to the guerrillas—ambushed a guerrilla column on the bank of the Grande river. Nine rebels died—among them Tania and Joaquín—and the only survivor, Paco, was wounded and taken prisoner. Che wrote in his diary about Joaquín: "He's an irreparable loss".

In September it was even worse. The army arrested 16 youths who worked as liaisons of the guerrillas in the city, among them Loyola Guzmán. A price was put on Che's head: 5000 dollars. In many places of the world there was disbelief that Guevara might really be in Bolivia. On the 26th, at La Higuera, near Vallegrande, Coco Peredo and Antonio (a veteran who had fought next to Che in the Sierra Maestra) were killed.

The beginning of the end

The last four days of September and the first three of October 1967 were tense for the guerrillas. Surrounded, decimated, without provisions, each day seemed like it would be the last.

Che wrote the last pages of his diary. Although he was weak and ravaged by asthma, he tried to keep the survivors' hopes high.

Sunday, October 8: There are 1800 soldiers in the outskirts of La Higuera. A peasant called Victor has discovered the guerrillas and reports their position to the Army. A special group of 180 rangers advances towards the El Yuro canyon. At 1.15 PM the final battle begins. Five hours later Che's dream comes to an end:

What happened next? Che's last hours are still a mystery. He was put away in a schoolhouse at La Higuera. An old woman brought him food. There was no death penalty in Boliva. But if Che lives, his captors fear that he will become a symbol for anyone who dreams of a better world. From La Paz comes an order that no Bolivian soldier shall ever admit having given or received: "Execute him".

On Monday morning of the 9th of October, Che—supposedly wounded—is transferred to Vallegrande in an army helicopter. He is leashed to the helicopter's skid, the worst place for transporting a wounded person. This increases the suspicions over his destination.

Monday the 10th of October of 1967, at noon, the Army staff headquarters officially confirms the death of Ernesto Che Guevara. The report says that his death was from "injuries received in combat". *Neither the press nor the international opinion believe this.* It will not be long before it is known that Guevara was shot to death—a helpless prisoner in the school at La Higuera—by sergeant Mario Terán. CIA (Central Intelligence Agency) Eduardo González was in charge of checking out the command.

The body was exhibited in a laundry room at Vallegrande's hospital. The photograph of Che's bullet-ridden corpse would become one of most dramatic of the 20th century. The following day the corpse vanishes from sight. Officially it was said that it had been cremated. Only his hands were saved, for identification. On the 16th of October, in La Habana, Fidel Castro announced: "The news of the death of Commander Ernesto Guevara is painfully true".

Eternal life

In the years following his death Che turned into a symbol for the youth, for the underdeveloped countries, for the dreamers of utopias who want to make the world a fairer place. He will be remembered for saying:

"A REVOLUTIONARY IS MOTIVATED BY LOVE AND NOT BY HATE. IF I WERE TO ACT UNDER THE INFLUENCE OF HATE I WOULD ONLY BE A MERCENARY."

"I FEEL A REPULSION FOR MONEY. IT'S A FUCKING FETISH."

On the 18th of October of 1967, in front of hundreds of people at the Revolution Square in La Habana, Fidel Castro would say of him:

HOW DO WE WANT THE MEN OF THE FUTURE GENERATIONS TO BE? MAY THEY BE LIKE THE CHE! HOW DO WE WANT OUR CHILDREN TO BE EDUCATED? MAY THEY BE EDUCATED IN THE SPIRIT OF THE CHE!

Julio Cortázar would write of him:

I had a brother
who roamed the mounts
while I slept.
I loved him my way
I took his voice from him
free as the water.
At times I walk
near his shadow.
We never met each other,
but it did not matter.
My brother awake
while I slept.
My brother showing me
after the night
his chosen star
while I slept.

At La Higuera the peasants would vindicate him as Saint Ernesto of La Higuera and turn the schoolhouse into a shrine. The year of Che's death, **Pope Paul VI** announced the Populorum Progressio (Development of Nations) encyclical, that says in one of its paragraphs:

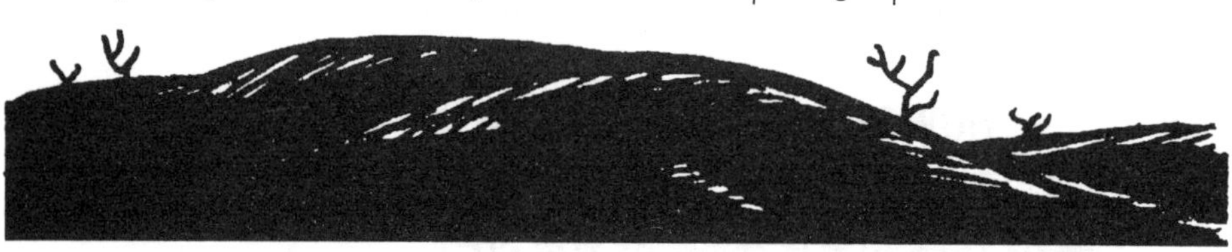

"The Earth has been created by God for all men. The right of property and free trade are subordinated to the fundamental right that each person has to avail himself what he needs. Upon the basic demands of common well-being no unconditional or absolute right of property exists. This is the reform that has to be fulfilled for fighting and defeating the injustice...."

Those who knew him would say that he loved poetry, that he read Goethe and Hegel, that he rejected honors, that he was capable of applying the same punishments to himself as on his subordinates when they did not do their jobs right, that he was shy and passionate, that he was ironic and fraternal, that he cherished altruism, that he was contemporary with the Beatles, the War of Vietnam, the attempts to reach the moon and that he transcended his time, with no other limits but eternity. Meanwhile, the names of his detractors and killers have fallen ingloriously into oblivion.

His five children—Hilda, Aleida, Camilo, Celia and Ernesto—receive as heritage a code-of-conduct, an attitude, a role-model and a letter that was handed to them after his departure.

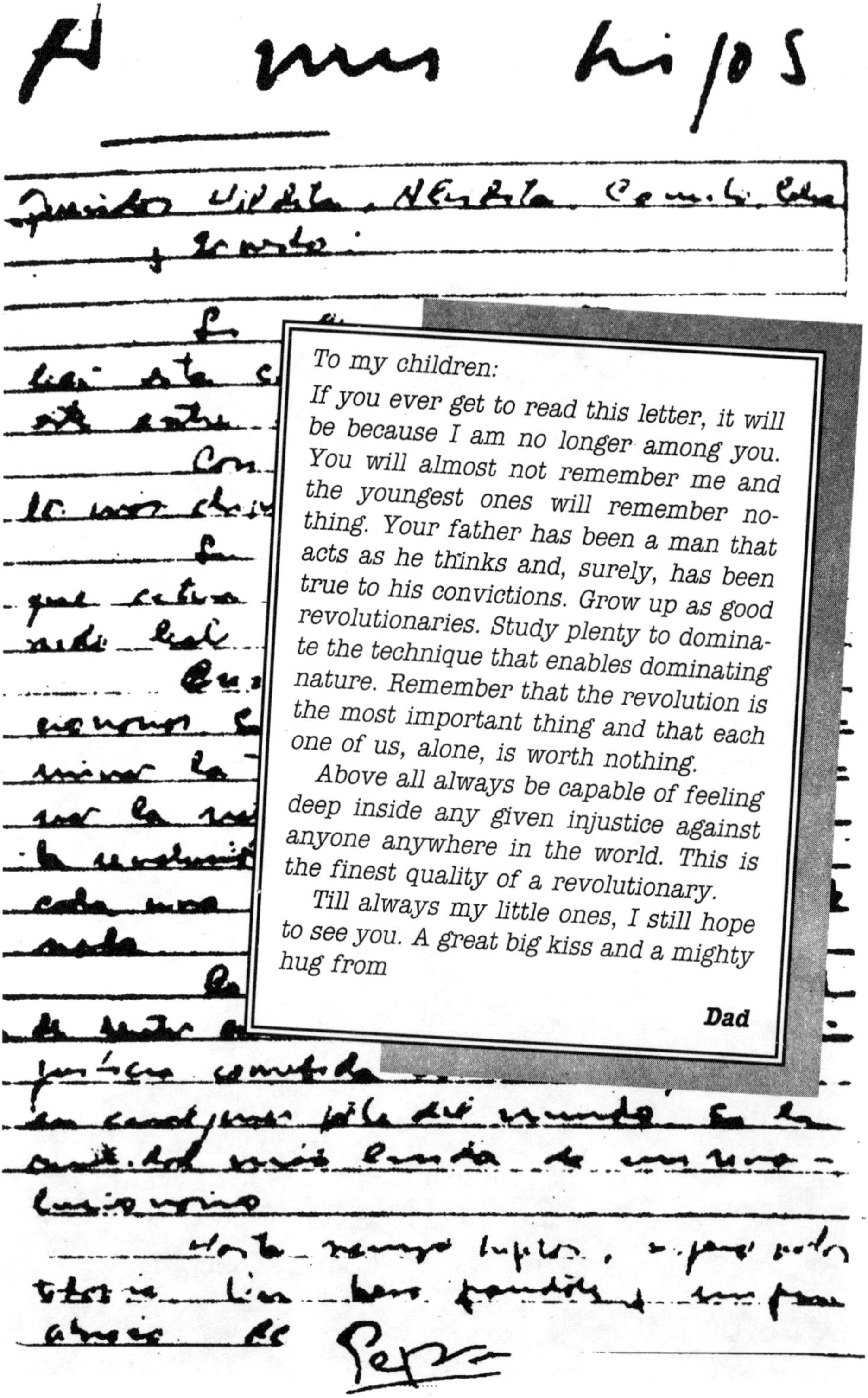

To my children:

If you ever get to read this letter, it will be because I am no longer among you. You will almost not remember me and the youngest ones will remember nothing. Your father has been a man that acts as he thinks and, surely, has been true to his convictions. Grow up as good revolutionaries. Study plenty to dominate the technique that enables dominating nature. Remember that the revolution is the most important thing and that each one of us, alone, is worth nothing.

Above all always be capable of feeling deep inside any given injustice against anyone anywhere in the world. This is the finest quality of a revolutionary.

Till always my little ones, I still hope to see you. A great big kiss and a mighty hug from

Dad

Vallegrande, Bolivia, 1996

Six months after having started, the task of the soldiers, anthropologists and forensics experts continues. New remains are found. Up to now, five corpses have been uncovered, reconstructed and identified. The bodies are those of guerrilla men who, thirty years earlier, had intended a new destiny for Latin America.

However, none of them is the one they are after: Che Guevara. The team, made up of Cuban, Argentinian and Bolivian experts began to look for him after that, on November of 1995, retired General Mario Vargas Salinas, one of they who fought the guerrilla, would say Che was not cremated. Another survivor, Gary Prado Salmón, agreed with him:

"THE EXECUTION WAS DECIDED BY THE GENERALS RENE BARRIENTOS, ALFREDO OVANDO CANDIA (COMMANDER OF THE ARMED FORCES) AND JUAN TORRES (CHIEF OF STAFF). AND AFTER THEY KILLED HIM, THEY ORDERED THAT HIS HANDS BE CUT OFF AND THAT HE BE BURIED IN A COMMON GRAVE".

The three generals exist only as three sad names in the history of Latin American military coups. Meanwhile, the people of Vallegrande are moved by the search for the remains; from all over America come—lured by curiosity and memory—hundreds of people.
There is a rally in the village:

As we near the end of the century, Che is the subject of new books, new biographies, new movies. His own works are readapted over and over again. Some look for his body, others for his ideas, others intend to redeem his model of life.

The Latin America that he dreamed of changing, keeps on being an unjust continent. A UN report released on the 15th of July of 1996 says that in the last thirty years (the time past since Che's death), the income of 20% of the poorest people in the planet fell from 2.3 to 1.4% of the world income.

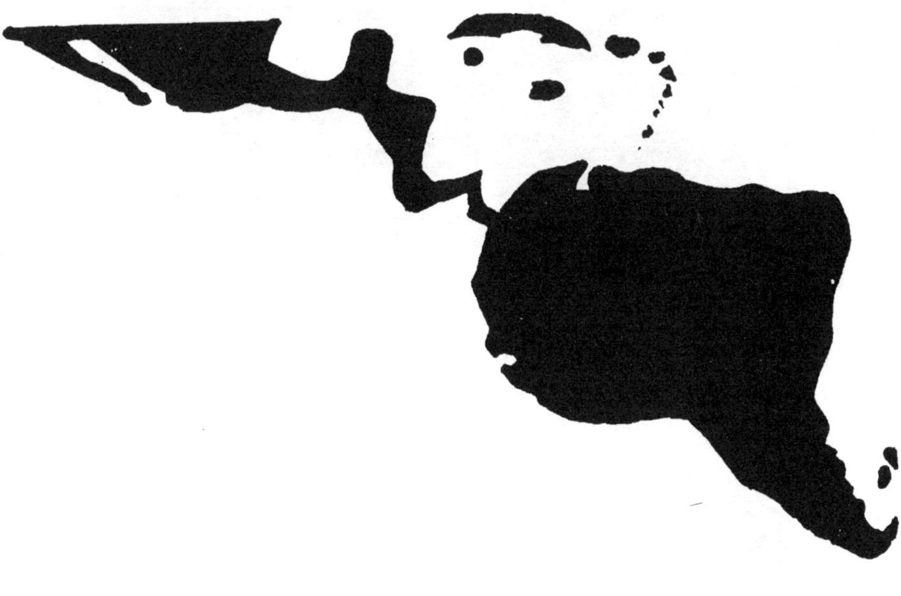

Over the political quarrels, beyond the misunderstandings, Che's figure gains recognition and respect within the perspective of time. Those who were his contemporaries as well as the new generations recognize him for: his integrity, his honesty, his solidarity, those characteristics that—in the last final years of the century—seem as scarce as they are necessary.

One of his biographers, Mexican **Paco Ignacio Taibo II**, writes:

"Ernesto Guevara shall be the last of our beloved heroes on horse-back (or on mule, or on donkey, the same goes for a man who was capable of laughing at himself), of the heroic tradition of Latin America."

Guide to names, institutions and ideas

ALLIANCE FOR PROGRESS: Organization created under John F. Kennedy's inspiration with the purpose of promoting the development of Latin America in accordance with US designs. Cuba was excluded from this scenario. The ALP failed with no pity or glory.

BARRIENTOS, RENÉ: Bolivian military, he headed the junta that overthrew President Paz Estenssoro and usurped power in 1964. In 1966 he retained it through elections. During his rule (distinguished for consenting to all American directives) Che's guerrillas entered the country and were defeated. Barrientos died in 1969, at age 50, in an airplane accident.

DEBRAY, REGIS: French philosopher and writer who met Che in La Habana in 1965 and went with him deeply into the Theory of the Focus. Debray joined the guerrillas in Bolivia in March 1967, with the nom de guerre of "Dantón". Che considered him "a good writer and a lousy guerrilla". On April 21 he left the guerrillas by mutual agreement with Che, was arrested by the Bolivian army and put on trial in Camirí. Back in France, in the 80's he was a government official during Francois Mitterand's rule. His post-guerrilla writings were always critical, his personal stands were never clear enough and even today he writes once again about that one experience, though these texts have not contributed to clarifying his ideas or explaining his actions.

EISENHOWER, DWIGHT DAVID: US republican president, between 1953 and 1961. As general of the American Army he was the supreme chief of the Allied Forces on the Normandy invasion in 1944 that ended with the defeat of Nazism. During his government the rebel movement started in Cuba and too, during his mandate, Fidel Castro assumed charge.

FOCUS (THEORY OF): Armed struggle strategy inspired by Che, according to which combat against a regime to be overthrown starts with the installation of a revolutionary "focus" (preferably rural) integrated by well-trained guerrillas, that as they attack objectives gain the population's confidence and support. According to Che, the rebels of that one focus should attack and retreat causing casualties and damages, without ever presenting frontal battle against the regular armies. This theory deviated into foquismo, a tactic adopted in the 60's and 70's by armed groups in Argentina, Uruguay, Brazil, Chile and Peru. The mechanical application of Che's ideas, without taking into consideration the social, political and even geographical conditions plus confusing a fighting tactic with a political strategy deviated into messianic positions with tragic consequences for numerous Latin American political militants.

FRONDIZI, ARTURO: Argentine president between 1958 and 1962. He ran for office as candidate for the Intransigent Radical Civil Union (UCRI), detached from the Radical Civic Union (UCR), after winning the elections in which Peronism was proscribed. He tried to establish a development policy and was overthrown by a military coup, partly because of his secret meeting with Che. He died in 1995, at 87, after having shifted to more and more conservative ideas.

GRANMA: Name of the small ship by which the first group of revolutionaries reached Cuba lead by Fidel and Raúl Castro, among whom there was only one foreigner: Che. The boat (named after a southeastern Cuban province) is now at the Museum of the Revolution, in La Habana.

NEW MAN: Concept launched by Che Guevara in writings and speeches to characterize the kind of human being that should result from the revolutionary environment. It envisioned a man who would not be guided by material interests, with a new ethic and new attitudes, distinct "from the were-wolf of the wolves' society". According to Che's writings, the New Man "does not have the desperate urge to steal from his peers, since man's exploitation of man has disappeared."

ILLIA, ARTURO UMBERTO: President of the Republic of Argentina, after winning, as the Radical Civic Union candidate, the elections of 1963. His was an austere government, with an orderly economic administration and a firm defense of national interests (especially in the oil and drugs areas) that brought on constant and growing pressures from the US. This Cordobean physician, of profound democratic convictions and attitudes, was overthrown by a military coup that general Juan Carlos Onganía headed in 1966. Illia died in 1983, at 83, after living in a modest way in the practice of his profession. Onganía, who threatened to rule for twenty years on the terms of hard authoritism (under his mandate, the University of Buenos Aires was destroyed during the "night of the long sticks"), was overthrown in 1970 by another general, Marcelo Levingston. During Illia's rule the army pressed so that the relations with Cuba would not be resumed.

JOHNSON, LYNDON BAINES: Vice-president of the US, who became president in 1963, upon the assassination of John F. Kennedy. He was re-elected in 1964 and concluded his term in 1969. The most noteworthy aspects of his term were that he compromised his country in the Vietnam War, increased the military aggression in Indochina and, along with the military commands that accompanied him, became the architect of the greatest military defeat in American history. He also maintained the blockade on Cuba and the hostility towards the government of La Habana. He died in 1973, at the age of 65.

KENNEDY, JOHN FITZGERALD: Democrat president of the US, between 1960 and 1963. On November 23 of that year he was murdered in Dallas, at 46. Officially, the crime was attributed to Lee Oswald, but multiple clues suggest a conspiracy prepared by powerful conservative business and political sectors. Kennedy promoted the civil rights of the blacks and committed himself not to invade Cuba in exchange that the Soviet Union remove its missiles from the island.

KHRUSHCHEV, NIKITA SERGEIEVICH: Prime minister of the Soviet Union between 1958 and 1964. During his mandate he denounced the crimes of his predecessor, Josef Stalin, and promoted, in the international scene, peaceful coexistence. Before being overthrown (and replaced by Leonid Brezhnev), his agrarian policy failed and he committed himself with Kennedy to remove the nuclear missiles from Cuba in exchange that the US would not invade the island.

MAO, TSE TUNG (or Zedong): Founder of the Chinese Communist Party in 1921, he led the struggle against the nationalist sec-

tors of his country through "The Long March", featuring tens of thousands of peasants, that connected Kiangsi with Yunan. In 1937 he made a pact with the nationalists to defeat together the Japanese invasion and later overcame his occasional allies in a civil war that lasted four years (1945-49). He proclaimed the People's Republic of China and was designated chairman. He criticized the USSR and, since 1957, organized a Marxist regime with characteristics of its own (from a peasant basis before one of blue-collar and city workers). Strong dogmatism and an emphatic personality cult stained his rule, that continued to 1976, when he died at the age of 83. He imposed the Cultural Revolution in 1976, a bloody movement destined to eliminate all signs of opposition, independent thought and bourgeois ways. All access to occidental and bourgeois production (music, literature, art, theater) was prohibited, thousands of people were executed; at schools, factories and universities the repetition of Maoist dogmas was obligatory. "The red book"(quotes and dogma), "About the lingering war" and "Of the practice" count among his works. Mao tried to recruit Che so that in Cuba he could impose the Chinese position instead of the Soviet.
Che refused and defended autonomy at any cost.

MARTÍ, JOSÉ: Emblematic figure of the Cuban independence. He was a politician, a writer, a poet and a lawyer. He was born in a poor family and, due to his tenacious struggle for the independence suffered prison and exile repeatedly. He lived in Spain, Guatemala, Mexico and New York. He practiced journalism, was a university professor and became one of the Latin American modernism pioneers. Among his most well-known works are "Simple Verses, Free Verses, Fatal Friendship" and the novel "The Golden Age". He founded the Cuban Revolutionary Party and died in combat at Playitas, eastern Cuba, in 1895, after disembarking to fight against the Spaniards. He was 42 years old. Fidel Castro, Che and their rebel army fought inspired by the dreams of Martí.

ORGANIZATION OF THE AMERICAN STATES (OAS): Organization founded in Bogotá in 1948 to coordinate the continental country's foreign policies. It has usually been an organism guided by the US, according to its interests and the member countries showed, in that forum, an almost null freedom of criterion. Cuba was expelled from the organization.

OVANDO CANDIA, ALFREDO: Bolivian coup military, he featured the coups against presidents Paz Estenssoro (1964) and Siles Salinas (1969). In his turn he was overthrown in 1970 by General Miranda. Chief of the General Staff when Che was captured, he and the generals Barrientos and Juan José Torres decided the execution of Guevara. He died in 1982, at 63.

PENTAGON: Name by which the headquarters of the US Armed Forces (Defense Department) is called due to the shape of the building that was constructed in Arlington, close to Washington, in 1941. The greater part of US foreign policy is decided in the Pentagon.

ROJO, RICARDO: A lawyer and a political writer, he met Che in 1953, in Bolivia, and from then on became one of his most affectionate friends. He formed part of a generation of utopian, rebellious and belligerent

youths, constituted in the heat of the University Reform of 1918. Close aid of Arturo Frondizi when he left the Radical Party in 1957, he was also a friend of Raúl Alfonsín, Fidel Castro and Salvador Allende. He testified on his bond with Che in the book "My friend Che", first published in 1968, that sold more than a million copies and was translated to fifteen languages.
He died when he was 72, in February of 1996.

SIERRA MAESTRA: Mountain chain that rises in the middle of the Cuban territory that separates the western and eastern regions of the Island. Sylvan with tropical vegetation, the Turquino peak, 5,922 feet high, marks its maximum elevation. In the Sierra Maestra were the Rebel Army's headquarters and that quest gave birth to legends, poems, stories, songs and an entire profuse revolutionary iconography.

TORRES, JUAN JOSÉ: Bolivian coup-liking military, one the three who took the decision of executing Che. He was president in 1970-71 and intended a populist policy with certain vindications for the miners and peasants. Overthrown by another coupist (General Hugo Bánzer) he went into exile and was assassinated in Argentina in 1976, at 57.

URRUTIA, MANUEL: He was revolutionary Cuba's first president, following Fidel Castro and his men's take of power. A lawyer and a politician, Urrutia defended Castro when he was tried during Fulgencio Batista's dictatorship. As president, he denounced the Cuban Communist Party's growing interference, which hastened his resignation a few months later (replaced by Osvaldo Dorticós) and his subsequent exile in 1963. He died in 1981, at the age of 80.

VIETNAM: Country in southeast Asia, situated in the peninsula of Indochina. Its coasts face the Sea of Meridian China. Its history begins in the 3rd century BC and is crossed by repeated intents of conquest on the part of China, Portugal (16th century), France (19th century), Japan (1941-45) and Cambodia (after 1978). In 1905 began the struggle for independence, under the charge of the Vietminh, a popular forces' front commanded by Ho Chi Minh (founder of the Indochinese Communist Party). Independence was proclaimed September 2 of 1945. It was not recognized by France and that brought about the war of Indochina that ended in 1954 upon the defeat of the French. Two countries were formed: the Democratic Republic of Vietnam (North Vietnam), with a communist regime, and the Republic of Vietnam (South Vietnam), with a pro-Occidental capitalist regime. They were to be unified through elections, according to the agreements celebrated in Geneva in 1954. This did not happen and originated a war between both regimes: the War of Vietnam. The US supported Southern Vietnam with money, troops and armaments and had an active participation in the war. The North resisted through a guerrilla army (the Vietcong), wherein men, women and children participated, always inspired by Ho Chi Minh's thoughts. Although the US displayed in Vietnam its maximum military power and a technology with an enormous lethal capacity, in 1975, after the defeat it was obligated to retreat. After the defeat of the South, both territories were fused and (in June of 1960) was created the Socialist Republic of Vietnam, presided by Ton Duc Thang, with Pham Van Dong as Prime Minister. All this process ran parallel to the Cuban revolution's fight for its own survival.

...UNTIL THE VICTORY,
FOREVER!

Bibliography

Adams, Jerome R. *Latin American Heroes.* New York: Ballantine Books, 1991.

Anderson, Jon Lee. *Che. A Revolutionary Life.* Grove Press, 1977.

Guevara, Ernesto Che. Trans. Carlos P. Hansen and Andrew Sincalir. *Bolivian Diary.* New York: Pathfinder, 1994.

____ . *Che Guevara and the Cuban Revolution: Writings and Speeches of Ernesto Che Guevara.* New York: Pathfinder/Pacific & Asia, 1987.

____ . *Episodes of the Cuban Revolutionary War.* New York: Pathfinder, 1996.

Harris, Richard L. *Death of a Revolutionary: Che Guevara's Last Mission.* W.W. Norton & Co., Inc., 1970.

Hodges, Donald C. *The Legacy of Che Guevara: A Documentary Study.* London: Thames & Hudson, 1977.

Prado Salmon, Gen. Gary. *The Defeat of the Che Guevara.* Westport, Conn.: Greenwood Press, 1990.

"Where is Che Guevara Buried? A Bolivian Tells," by Jon Lee Anderson. *The New York Times,* November 21, 1995.

Index

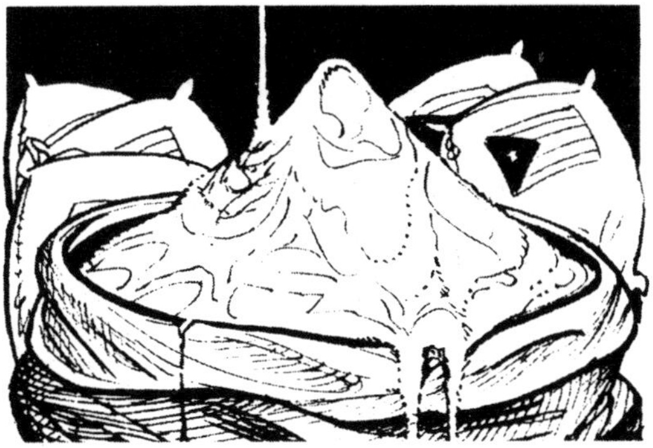